The Butterfly

Icon of the dream achiever

S Afrose

Ukiyoto Publishing

All global publishing rights are held by

Ukiyoto Publishing

Published in 2023

Content Copyright © S Afrose

ISBN 9789359208671

*All rights reserved.
No part of this publication may be reproduced,
transmitted, or stored in a retrieval system, in any form
by any means, electronic, mechanical, photocopying,
recording or otherwise, without the prior permission of
the publisher.*

The moral rights of the authors have been asserted.

*This is a work of fiction. Names, characters, businesses,
places, events, locales, and incidents are either the
products of the author's imagination or used in a fictitious
manner. Any resemblance to actual persons, living or
dead, or actual events is purely coincidental.*

*This book is sold subject to the condition that it shall not by
way of trade or otherwise, be lent, resold, hired out or
otherwise circulated, without the publisher's prior
consent, in any form of binding or cover other than that in
which it is published.*

www.ukiyoto.com

Dedicated to all the people
For achieving their sweet dreams.
To decorate their beautiful wards
As like as the butterflies.

Acknowledgement

Thanks a lot Dear Almighty for blessing me always.

Thank you so much dear parents, friends, readers.

Without yours' supports, I can't make my staircase, to achieve the sweet dream.

Due to those lovely drops upon my arts, they get the spiritual power to fly; as like as the butterflies. Yes! My dreamy butterflies.

Love for all, from the deepest core of my heart.

From Author Desk
© S Afrose
Dhaka, Bangladesh, 15th Sep-23.

Hold On For Some Moments

A special fragrance is here. What's that? Who can give the answer? Who will play that role? Please! It's essential to know.

A blooming flower! It's the dearest life. It will be the beloved hub at last.

How and when? As there are so many strikes. Hopes can't stuck anymore. They are fading gradually. Then, how will it be a lovely life?

It's not like that. Life is beautiful at each step. Life is the platform of game. We must think positively. We will be the winners of the desired games at last. Each step has such a unique value, that makes the footprint, as a sign of love. Just need to accept this and access the way with positive thoughts.

Look at the Caterpillar. How miserable its life! Nobody loves. But it doesn't give up. After the painful phase of life, the dreamy phase is arrived. And it's happened very soon. Just Patience! Really?

Yes! That's true. Transformation, from one stage to another, of the life; finally that turns into the cute

Butterfly. How wonderful! Everyone loves the butterfly.

Don't worry. It will be fine. Never mind. Life swings always. Just stop for a while for taking the break and then go ahead. Imprint that image of Butterfly in the mind's canvas. **That butterfly is the icon of the dream achiever.**

You will be able to see the bluish sky, all the time.

Love and pain, sorrowness and happiness...whatever; we must accept all states of the life heartfully. All are essential to maintain the rhythms of the life.

'The Butterfly'*- it is ready as a rider; the dream catcher, the dream achiever.*

This poetry book contains so many writes, spreading the essence of life's states.

For example-**The beautiful butterfly, The miserable life, For the cute ride, Transformation of life etc**

Hold this book and spend some nice moments as the dearest friend. Hope, you will like and enjoy the time; will get a special fragrance and able to be the dream catcher-Butterfly. I think it would be. For any kind of unexpected word, just forgive.

May Almighty bless all of us!

Thanks!
From Author desk.
©S Afrose
Bangladesh
15th Sep-23

What Is This Butterfly?

The dream achiever from its poor state to a stable one.

How can it happen?

"Without losing hope, hold on the rope of dreamy kite"

Then it will fly one day, from ground to sky.

"From the Caterpillar to the Butterfly"

> "Life is full of ups-downs.
> Need to be honest
> To itself,
> By the knot of hope & trust;
> For achieving the dreamy wings
> To fly high."

"Let's start,
The awesome journey.
The magic of words
For all of us,
Let's enjoy"

© S Afrose

Contents

The Beautiful Butterfly	1
Just An Insect	2
The Miserable Life	3
Believe In Dear God	4
Butterfly	5
For The Cute Ride	6
That Last Sip	7
That Corner Shelf	8
What's That Key?	10
Your Favourite Dish	12
The Flying Fish	13
The Peacock	15
Transformation Of Life	16
The Life	18
Resurrection Of Beautiful Mind	20
A New Trail	22
Mark Your Each Movement	23
See The Letter	25
Listen The Song	26
Sound Of That Bell	27

The Tree	29
Some Signs	31
Fantastic	33
Like As The Newborn	34
Shower	36
The Dramatic Change	37
Miserable Rain	38
Little Butterfly	39
Daring Part	41
The Paper Said	42
Meeting	43
B For Beautiful	44
B For Beast	45
Life Will Touch	46
Any Permission?	47
Kingdom Of Butterflies	48
The Game	49
That's You	51
Outstanding Pleasure	53
The Pocket	54
The Boat	55
The Tiger	57

Must Know The Fact	58
The Last Verse	59
Thinking Hopefully	60
Close Those Timid Eyes	62
The Bird Of Life	63
The Morning Dew	65
The Biggest Portrait	66
The Biggest Dream	67
Do Or Not	69
No Entry	70
Make It Powerful	71
Beside The Garden	72
Cranes Of Love	73
Finally	74
About the Author	76

The Beautiful Butterfly

Hello my dear friends,
Let's enjoy this lane.
The beautiful ride
Of the butterfly.

The beautiful butterfly!
Within all of us,
We forget to search,
This is not fair.

The beautiful butterfly!
It plays, it flies.
Let's enjoy with it,
The trend of life.

The Butterfly

Just An Insect

It's here.
Oh no!
What is this?

Just an insect.
A Caterpillar!
Yes.

It's the Caterpillar.
A simple art
Of this earth.

Just an insect
Midst the nature.
How wondrous!

The Miserable Life

So miserable the life.
Day to night
Can't bear,
The same tear;
Always fear.
Ah!

So miserable
The life.
How can rectify?
How can recover,
From this part?
Need a magical mart.

Believe In Dear God

Don't stop
Praying,
To dear God.

Believe in dear God!

He is the only one hope.
He will help-
He will bless.

Believe in dear God!

You can't lose the hope.
You must believe this,
You will be the winner at last.

Butterfly

After so many days,
A new dawn,
A new hope;
A new dream.

Butterfly!
The cute butterfly!
Wow!
Unbelievable.

After so many painful tears,
The song of lovely life can hear.
These guys,
For your love, dear.

The cute butterfly!
The lovely butterfly!

For The Cute Ride

A new knot,
For the cute vault.

A new rite,
For the cute ride

Don't make any mistake.
Careful!

The beautiful ride of life,
It's waiting for you.

The cute and lively ride,
Need to accept nicely dear.

That Last Sip

The coffee mug!
The coffee table!

The same window,
The same weather.

Except the time,
When you passed away.

The last sip
Of the coffee,

It remains the same.
The essence of the sweet moment.

Then why don't you understand,
The game of life?

That Corner Shelf

The room
Is empty.

The time
Is not compatible.

That person
Is not here.

He is different.
She is different.

What's the identity?
What's the identity?

That corner shelf,
Holding lots of books.
Past to present-

Try to look, one by one.

Then do you regret?
Transaction is lying.

What's That Key?

It will,
It must be.

After the winter,
Golden moon arrives.

Golden nature dances.
Golden nature sings.

Where is the key?

Searching!

Day to night.
Day to month.

Month to year
Year goes on as usual.

Where is the key?

Can't find out?

What's that key?
May I ask?

The key of love.
The key happiness.

Is that right?
Then don't panic anymore.

Search instantly.

Inside your mind.

Your Favourite Dish

Take this meal
Your favourite dish.

For sound health,
You love it.

Take this meal
The pen and the poetry.

For the sound mind
Mystic happiness!

The Flying Fish

There's a flying fish.
So rush, a dish.

There's a flying kite.
Rush, for what?

The fish is
In the pond,

The fish says
Hello dear friend.

What do you want?
My riding can trace.

The flying kite
Not so far.
You cry

The Butterfly

I don't mind.

Patience!
For the success.

Will be happy

You must agree with that.

The flying fish.
The flying kite.

Similar?
Of course.

We make our rides
Whatever the weather.

The Peacock

The rainy day!
Mind is happy.
Heart is lost,
Towards the wonderful plot.

The Pen
On the rain,
The mind
On its ride.

The beautiful ride!
The pen with drops of love,
From the heaven.
Not expected, ever.

The peacock comes
From the dearest mind,
Though it was lost
On the graveyard.

Transformation Of Life

Transformation of life,
From one stage to another.

Dear life!
You must wait for the desired time.

Transformation of life,
From painful to happiness shower.

Dear life!
You will revive that beautiful smile.

Look at the butterfly,
So cute.

How does it come?
From the phase of Caterpillar's life.

The lovely stage of Butterfly's life.
That's the transformation.

Tuning the rhythms,
At any condition.

As you know,
This is the temporary shell of life.
Your dreamy staircase is waiting ahead.
You must chase.

You must be the dream catcher.
You must be the dream achiever.

The Life

The life!
Still the dearest one.

The life!
Still the sweet pie.

The life!
Still the haunted past.

The life!
Still the dreamy kite.

The life
Is the vast canvas.

Hold the bush and colour pellets,
Sketch all the beautiful images.

The life
Is the pool of love.

The life
Is full of dangers.

So what?
You are the owner of that canvas.
Remember.
Make the new portrait again.

You will see,
There's the smiley hub of the life.

Resurrection Of Beautiful Mind

For a long,
Sober!

For a long,
Hopeless!

For a long,
Dancer.

For a long,
Broken heart.

For a long,
Upset!

For a long,
Lost happiness!

How can survive?
Resurrection of love.

Resurrection of each part,
Which is the fundamental art.

Resurrection of beautiful mind.
Hahahahaha!
Sound of mind!
Beats of heart!

Now they are here.
Where are you, dear?

A New Trail

The magic reel!
The magic seal!

The magic tracker!
The magic trail!

When river flows,
When Zephyr plays,

Nature sings.
Wave dances.

Can see something,
Can't feel something?

A new trail!
It's omnipotent.

Mark Your Each Movement

Nothing is going on,
As per the mind's role.

Come on dear,
We can share.

Why don't see,
The sky or sun or moon?

Because they are always there,
Your dreamy universe.

You are there.
You have to realise.

You can't wait.
Why, so rush?

The Butterfly

Mark your each movement
On the canvas of earth.

See The Letter

Some words,
Some lines,

A quote!

Some lines,
Some arts,

A poem!

See the letter
For you,
Was here.

A message,
A case,
You deserve.

Listen The Song

Listen the song.
Feel the tone.
Feel the core point.

Listen the song.
Everywhere, every time.
Feel the hidden emotions.

To your heart,
The beautiful art.
What's that?

Your dream!
Your love!
Your life!

That's true.
You forget.
So listen, the song.

Sound Of That Bell

River wishes- Oh God!
Let me flow always,
For the flowery lane.

Let me flow,
To drench each sorrow
Of any person.

River wishes
To God,
For its evergreen heart.

A sound heard
From so far,
That must be a bell.

Sound of that bell,
Helps to open

The Butterfly

The closed eyes.

Then can make,
The wishes
On the prayer time.

Sound of that bell,
Inside the deepest shell
Of the mind.

As the flowing river,
You must realise,
You are the floating rider.

The Tree

A long tree
Is here.

So many trees,
Were in that past.

The vacancy,
For what?

No more trees.
How pathetic!

A long night!
Tree cries.

People,
This is not right.

The Butterfly

You need to care
Each of your dearest arts.

We belong there.
Why don't you care?

Some Signs

There are some signs
    Of the step.

Your footprints,
On the lap of the earth.

Look at there, carefully.
    What's that?

Some are vanished.
You can't recollect.

What can you learn?
    Trying again.

Make the steps,
On the people's minds.

The Butterfly

Some signs appear,
Those are lovely petals.

They will be showered always,
As the perpetual parts.

Fantastic

Just wow!
Heart loves.
Mind says-
Crazy, you're!

Heart says-
Fantastic!
Mind says-
What?

"The world is not for love.
It wants only wealth and pride."

Really?
Not at all.

Some live as those blind ones,
Truth is love, the golden sunshine!

Like As The Newborn

Make the castle
Of your own.

Like as the newborn,
Only happiness and joy.

Make the castle
Of your dream.

Like as the newborn,
Dreamy swing.

Make the castle
Of dear dreams.

Like as the newborn,
Gradually hear the ringtone.

Love you dear.
Sweet life!

Shower

Take your shower
Beneath the azure's heart.

With colourful snowballs,
With love and love.

Take your shower,
Wash away all darts.

Those hold bad smell.
Just need the new essence.

After this essence,
Spread it.

The dreamy essence is everywhere.
The dreamy mart!

The Dramatic Change

Nobody can guess,
When
Life
Makes,
The dramatic change.

The beautiful stage,
Is onward.
On your way,
Just take your time.
Manage properly.

The dramatic change!
It's omnipotent.
To be there,
Playing as the player.
Strange!

Miserable Rain

Oh God!
Is this the life?
I forget,
When I smile
The last time.

Oh God!
Can't you help?
How strange!
It's me.
Ah!

Miserable rain!
Is that only for me?
I don't believe.
I need the casting role,
For achieving the goal.

Little Butterfly

Here a little butterfly.

It says- hi.

I am here.

Would you like to be here?

We will make a team,

For the wonderful game of life.

The little butterfly's trail.

So cute.
So sweet.
At last,
Mind agrees.

The Butterfly

Crippled mind
Now, is ready;
For the play time of life.

Daring Part

When you will
Face,
Any challenge;
Daring part,
You're
There.

Daring, you're!
Want to touch,
Peak of heaven,
Peak of mountain.
Mysterious!
Hidden dream catcher!

The Paper Said

Yesterday!
The paper said-
"I will not be with you"

You don't love me.
You use my heart,
To clean any dust.

Today!
The paper asking-
"Where are you?"

I want to be with you-
But there's nobody.

(14th Sep-23)

Meeting

A meeting
Over the phone
Hello!
Can hear?

A meeting
Can't be held.
The time runs,
Life stucks.

A meeting
Between two ones,
Heart & Mind.
The time?

A meeting
Most important,
To identify
The upcoming trend.

B For Beautiful

Beautiful bay!
Sanguine ray.

Beautiful sky.
Crimson vibes.

Beautiful mind,
Suddenly lost.

Upset for what?
Need to identify.

Beautiful life.
Why don't you come?

Shyness for what?
Loser, not a matter.

B For Beast

B for beast.
Human feast.

So dangerous.
Crippled stick.

Nest of beasts.
Beat to fix.

Least find out the gist.
Need to check this properly.

Life Will Touch

Life will touch
Ray of love.
If it wants
As like as the prayer.

Life will touch,
Topic for what?
Life will be trying,
For the universal art.

Life transfers,
Life blooms,
Nearby;
The boat of dreamy flies.

Any Permission?

Do you have any permission?
Who permits?
To go-
To do-
Just tell us.

We want,
To know,
To make,
A clear role;
Missing information, not allowed.

Any permission,
From dear self?
If not,
Then go to hell.
Just witness of the life's reel.

Kingdom Of Butterflies

There are
So many people,
So many eyes;
Except one art.

Kindly check.
What's that?
Kingdom of Butterflies!
As the flying race,
Need to be a part.

Any disclosure?
Any disguise?
Butterflies,
For you and I,
Dreamy port of life.

The Game

Choose the option.
The real captain!
The right caption!

For the game of life,
That's obviously right.
The game!

Reel of life
Can't hide,
It will come as the day light.

As a player,
Play dear.
Will learn so many arts.

Loser or not,
That's not a matter.

The Butterfly

Need to take the nap, at last.

A sweet roll,
For the goal
Of the game.

That's You

Forward Forcing!
Backward Forcing!

Oh!
Can't tolerate anymore.

Hey you!
Yes, that's you.

Have made the delusion.
Just calm down.

Come back in your sense.
Will get
A proper solution.

Crying as usual?
Not your part,

That's only, on the prayer time, to Almighty.

It's you,
Who can do anything,
If you believe dear.

Outstanding Pleasure

That cliff
Of the Mountain,
Everest or Himalayas;
A new venture,
Just chill.

Overall
You can't.
It's your fear,
Acts as a killer,
For your dream.

Yes dear,
Cliff is clearly seen.
Way is dancing
Onward,
Just chill, outstanding pleasure.

The Pocket

The pocket is full
Taking all rules.

The pocket is teared.
Rules are fallen petals.

Now feeling relax.
Your voice of heart-

Go on,
Make your own ride.

As the Butterfly
Enjoy the entire ride of life.

(16th Sep-23)

The Boat

The bosom of earth!
The bosom of sea!

A tiny boat!
Only I, with my dream.

The wave comes,
Holding my arms.

The dream scares.
I dare,
To say boldly.

Go on,
From this site.
This is my part.

I don't want to fight with you.

The Butterfly

I am here,
Searching my butterfly.

The Tiger

See that art
The tiger of life.
The tiger of your mind!
The tiger of your heart!

That's not appropriate,
Always dear.

See here
Or look at there.

The tiger is the part,
Of your dearest life.

Make the part.
Make the art.
Make the cosmic sight,
Make the knot of love.

Must Know The Fact

Must know the fact.
The news of life
So tough,
To digest.

The fact is here,
Accept it with love.
The news of heart,
The news of mind.

Hello universe!
Hold this part.
The new art,
The new hut.

Be the part,
Be the art,
Be the friend
Of happiness.

The Last Verse

The last verse
Of life.

The last time
Of dream.

It will arrive
Very soon or later.

You will not aware.
What can you do?

The last verse of life
Is here,

Now what can you do?
Escape, how?

Thinking Hopefully

Sitting there
A new layer.

A new vision
A new trend.

What can you see?
What can you do?

Thinking hopefully,
Thoughts be there.

May be not so easy,
May be not so good.

Thinking hopefully,
Will be there,

Go to bed,
Sweet nap, a new state.

Close Those Timid Eyes

Close those timid eyes.
They have no right,
To open
To see,
The sight of heart.

Close those timid eyes.
They are not right,
To fight
To make,
The bridge of life.

Those are here.
Rare and share.
Never dare,
To say,
Who is there?

The Bird Of Life

Once upon a time,
A tiny life.
A tiny bird!

The bird is where?
The bird is rare.

The bird of life!
Once upon a time,
The bird of life.

Lost property!
Lost priority!
Lost prospects of life.

The bird of life
So mystic,
How can make your ride?

That may be,
The broken sense.
The lost palace of life!

The Morning Dew

Some, few more;
Some, few words;
Some, few drops;

The morning dew!
The morning club!
The morning cliff!
The morning starts.

Dew drops come
From its core,
With the soothing balm.
Never forget.

The morning dew,
Makes the call;
Give a seal,
Play the desired role.

The Biggest Portrait

When I was a little one,
Holding the hands
Of my mom.

The biggest portrait of life!

When I was a toddler,
Holding the hands
Of the father.

The biggest portrait of life!

When I was a younger one,
No one withstand with me.
What's?

The biggest portrait?
Life is moulding its fold.

The Biggest Dream

Give a ring.

See,
A seal,
A meal.

The biggest dream!

Parents' dream,
Will be
A great human being.

The biggest dream!

I will be the dream catcher.
The biggest dream of my life,
To be a great human being.

The Butterfly

I will fly,
With dreamy wings of mind;
My friend is butterfly.

Do Or Not

What do you think?
Do or not.

What is your goal?
Do or not.

What do you say?
Say or not.

Feel or not?
Just accept the role.

No Entry

Restricted zone?

For all.
No entry,
Without wearing,
The costume.

Restricted for all.

If you don't agree,
You will be held
As a captivate,
Into the jail.

The life
Then,
What can you do?
Restricted zone, ouch!

Make It Powerful

Make it possible.
Make it powerful.

Though you know
You can't.

Those are powerful.
Those are painful.

Though you don't know,
What will happen?

Make it powerful.
Your rules.

Your pool,
You have to know all things.

Beside The Garden

The same umbrella!
The same weather!
The same tune!

Beside the garden,
The new string.
The new tune!

The new song playing,
Beside the garden.
Do you know?

Of course,
Beside the garden,
A beautiful crane dances.

Cranes Of Love

Two of them,
Sing and dance.

Cranes of love,
For what?
For whom?

Two of them-
Song of love!
Song of heart!

Cranes of life,
For all of us.

Finally

Finally can see.
Can show
Platform of life.

The magic of ward.

Finally can show,
Can see
The ray of heart.

The magic of ward!
The magic of mind!
The magic of words!

**"THANK YOU SO MUCH
FOR YOUR LOVE,
TOWARDS MY TINY POETRY WORLD,
THE PARADISE OF WORDS."
© S AFROSE
BANGLADESH**

About the Author

S Afrose

Author S Afrose (Sabiha Afrose, from Bangladesh) has made her writing realm since August-2020. She enjoys each of the part of this writing ward. She tries to express the hidden word or emotion, by her words; with the glamour of poetry. Poetry is her best friend. Her writes have been published on magazines and anthologies. In this writing realm, she has achieved many awards (beyond her expectations eg. Doctorate in Literature from Instituto Cultural Colombiano, Literoma Laureate Winner 2022, Mahatma Gandhi Award 2023 from Instituto Cultural Colombiano etc.

Published author of poetry books- Thanks Dear God, Poetic Essence, Reflection of Mind, Glittering Hopes,

Angels Smile, Tiny Garden of Words, Dancing Alphabet, Artistic Muse,

Essence of love, The Magical Quill, Dear Children, Haunted Site.

All are available worldwide (on Amazon.com & from publication hub). Apart these, there are some Bengali and English poetry books(available on rokomari.com in Bangladesh).

Her mother is Selina Begum and father is Manirul Islam.

Educational achievements- B Pharm, M Pharm from Jahangirnagar University, Bangladesh..

Contact- afrosewritings@outlook.com, sabiha_pharma@yahoo.com

You Tube: S Afrose *Muse of Writes*(@safrose_poetic_arts)

Facebook page: Muse of Words by S Afrose

Twitter:@afrose2020

Inst. @safrosepoetryworld

"Be the butterfly
   Fly so high
      Your desired ride."

www.ingramcontent.com/pod-product-compliance
Lightning Source LLC
LaVergne TN
LVHW041538070526
838199LV00046B/1731